The Scrumptious Scones Cookbook

Irresistible Scone Recipes for Every Occasion

While every precaution has been taken in the preparation of this book, the publisher assumes no responsibility for errors or omissions, or for damages resulting from the use of the information contained herein.

THE SCRUMPTIOUS SCONES COOKBOOK

First edition. January 13, 2024.

ISBN: 979-8224305100

Written by john ahmad.

Table of Contents

John Ahmad

Chapter 1: The Art of Scone Making

Understanding Scone Basics

Scones, with their inviting golden crust and tender interior, are a timeless treat that brings comfort and delight to countless tables. To embark on a journey of scone creation, it's essential to first understand the foundational elements that transform simple ingredients into delectable pastries.

Scone Ingredients

At the heart of every scone recipe lie a handful of key ingredients, each playing a vital role in shaping the final product. Flour serves as the structure, providing the base that holds everything together. The type of flour you choose—whether all-purpose, self-rising, or whole wheat—will influence the texture and flavor of your scones.

Butter, with its rich and creamy consistency, not only contributes flavor but also plays a crucial role in creating the desired flakiness. As the butter melts during baking, it releases steam, causing the layers of dough to separate and create that sought-after airy texture.

Sugar adds sweetness and moisture, elevating the scone's taste and tenderness. Whether you opt for granulated sugar, brown sugar, or even honey, this sweet element is an essential part of the scone equation.

Liquid, usually in the form of milk or cream, binds the ingredients together and hydrates the dough. The amount of liquid used and the way it's incorporated can significantly impact the final texture.

The Scone Technique

Creating scone dough is a delicate process that involves achieving the right balance between mixing the ingredients and handling the dough.

Begin by combining the dry ingredients—flour, sugar, baking powder, and any desired seasonings—in a mixing bowl. Cut cold butter into small cubes and incorporate it into the dry mixture using a pastry cutter or your fingertips. The goal is to achieve a crumbly texture, with pea-sized pieces of butter distributed throughout the mixture.

Once the butter is integrated, add the liquid gradually while gently stirring. Overmixing can result in tough scones, so it's important to mix only until the dough comes together. Turn the dough out onto a floured surface and pat it into a disc. This is where the magic happens: the layers of butter and dough create the scone's characteristic flakiness.

Fold the dough gently, creating layers, and cut out your scones using a round cutter. Remember to press straight down and lift—avoid twisting the cutter, which could seal the edges and inhibit proper rising.

Essential Ingredients and Tools
Baking Staples

Understanding the roles of flour and leavening agents is essential. All-purpose flour is versatile and works well in most scone recipes. Self-rising flour contains baking powder and salt, making it convenient for quick scone preparation. Whole wheat flour adds nuttiness and nutrition, but it requires adjustments in liquid to maintain the right texture.

Baking powder and baking soda are the leavening agents responsible for the scone's rise. Baking powder provides immediate lift, while baking soda reacts with acidic ingredients to create gas bubbles, resulting in extra lightness.

Fat and Flavor

Butter is a star ingredient, creating flakiness and flavor. Ensure it's cold when incorporated, so it remains solid and creates pockets of steam during baking. Experiment with different fats like coconut oil for unique flavor profiles.

Sugar enhances taste and texture. Brown sugar adds depth, while honey imparts subtle sweetness and moisture. The right balance depends on the desired flavor profile.

Tools of the Trade

Gather essential tools such as mixing bowls, measuring cups, and spoons. A pastry cutter or two forks are excellent for cutting butter into the dry ingredients. Use a bench scraper to fold and lift dough gently during shaping.

Invest in a round biscuit cutter or simply use a sharp-edged glass for cutting out scones. A baking sheet lined with parchment paper ensures easy release and prevents sticking.

Tips for Perfect Texture and Flavor

The Role of Mixing

Balancing the mixing process is vital. Overmixing results in tough scones due to excess gluten development, while undermixing leads to uneven distribution of ingredients. Aim for a cohesive dough that's mixed just enough to combine the elements.

Handling Add-Ins

Add-ins like dried fruits, nuts, or chocolate chips contribute variety and texture. Fold them into the dough with care, ensuring they're distributed evenly without overworking the mixture.

Baking Time and Temperature

Preheat your oven to the temperature specified in the recipe. Properly preheated ovens ensure even baking and proper rise. Bake the scones until they're golden brown and have a hollow sound when tapped on the bottom. This indicates that the interior is cooked through.

With a solid grasp of scone basics, essential ingredients, and proper techniques, you're equipped to embark on your scone-making journey. This chapter has set the stage for creating scones that are not only visually enticing but also irresistibly delicious.

Chapter 2: Classic Plain Scones

Traditional Buttery Bliss

Classic plain scones are a testament to the simple yet exquisite nature of scone baking. With a few essential ingredients and a touch of finesse, these scones bring to life the true essence of scone-making.

The Quintessential Ingredients

At the heart of every classic plain scone is a handful of timeless ingredients. Begin with all-purpose flour, the versatile canvas upon which the scone's character is painted. Cold butter is a fundamental component, contributing to both flavor and texture. Choose high-quality unsalted butter and dice it into small cubes to ensure even distribution throughout the dough.

A subtle sweetness emerges from a modest amount of granulated sugar, just enough to enhance the scone's overall taste without overpowering its simplicity. Finally, the liquid element, often milk or cream, binds the ingredients together and hydrates the dough. opt for whole milk or heavy cream for the richest results.

The Art of Incorporation

Creating classic plain scone dough is a delicate dance that requires precision and care. Begin by whisking together the dry ingredients—flour, sugar, and a pinch of salt—in a large mixing bowl. Add the cold butter cubes and, using a pastry cutter or your fingertips, work the butter into the flour until the mixture resembles coarse breadcrumbs. This step is essential for achieving the sought-after flakiness that defines classic scones.

Next, it's time to incorporate the liquid. Pour it in gradually, stirring gently with a fork or a wooden spoon. The goal is to form a cohesive dough without overmixing. Overmixing can lead to tough scones, so stop as soon as the dough comes together.

Achieving the Perfect Flakiness

The secret to the flakiness that makes classic plain scones a delight lies in the layers of butter and dough. After forming the dough, turn it out onto a lightly floured surface. Gently pat it into a circle that's about an inch thick. Fold the dough in half, creating layers, then pat it down again. Repeat this process a few times to ensure the butter is distributed evenly and creates pockets of flakiness during baking.

When cutting out the scones, use a round biscuit cutter or a glass dipped in flour to prevent sticking. Press the cutter straight down into the dough without twisting to allow for proper rising in the oven. Place the cut scones on a baking sheet lined with parchment paper, leaving a bit of space between each to allow for expansion.

Serving Suggestions and Variations

Freshly Baked Bliss

The joy of classic plain scones is amplified when they emerge warm from the oven. The golden-brown exterior, slightly crisp to the touch, gives way to a tender interior. The fragrance of butter and flour fills the air, enticing anyone nearby with its irresistible aroma.

Clotted Cream and Jam

For the quintessential scone experience, serve classic plain scones with clotted cream and jam. Slather a scone with clotted cream, a thick and velvety dairy product with a slightly sweet flavor. Top it off with a dollop of your favorite jam or preserve, whether it's strawberry, raspberry, or apricot. The interplay of creamy richness and fruity sweetness creates a sublime balance of flavors.

Variations to Explore

While the allure of classic plain scones lies in their simplicity, don't hesitate to explore variations that enhance the experience. Add a handful of currants or raisins for bursts of sweetness and texture. Consider incorporating a touch of citrus zest—such as lemon or orange—to infuse the scones with a refreshing aroma. For those seeking a richer option, substitute part of the milk or cream with heavy cream, resulting in an even more luxurious scone.

Classic plain scones capture the essence of scone-making artistry. With just a handful of carefully selected ingredients and a mindful approach to technique, you can craft scones that embody buttery flakiness, tender crumb, and timeless appeal. Whether enjoyed warm from the oven or adorned with clotted cream and jam, these scones remain a tribute to the beauty of simplicity.

Chapter 3: Heavenly Fruit-Infused Scones

Bursting with Fresh Fruits

Heavenly fruit-infused scones are a vibrant celebration of the seasons, where the succulent essence of fresh fruits merges seamlessly with the delicate texture of scones. These scones encapsulate the pure, unadulterated joy of indulging in nature's sweet gifts.

Fresh Fruit Selection

When crafting fruit-infused scones, the selection of fresh fruits is paramount. Berries—juicy and bursting with flavor—are a popular choice. Whether it's the bold sweetness of strawberries, the rich tang of blueberries, the brightness of raspberries, or the complexity of blackberries, each brings its unique charm to the scone canvas. Stone fruits like peaches, apricots, and plums lend a luscious juiciness that harmonizes with the scone's crumbly perfection. Citrus fruits, such as oranges and lemons, add a zesty and invigorating twist.

Incorporating Fresh Fruits

When integrating fresh fruits into scone dough, take care to prepare them properly. Wash, dry, and dice the fruits to your desired size. To prevent excess moisture, pat the fruit dry with a paper towel. Gently fold the fruit into the dough, ensuring an even distribution without crushing the fruit pieces.

As fresh fruits introduce additional moisture, it's wise to adjust the liquid content of the dough. If the dough becomes overly wet, incorporate a touch more flour. The objective is to maintain the dough's consistency while embracing the burst of fresh fruit.

Dried Fruits for Depth of Flavor

Dried fruits contribute a depth of flavor and chewy texture that complements the scone's crumbly structure. Their concentrated sweetness and intensified taste create delightful bursts of flavor throughout each scone. Dried cranberries, raisins, currants, and chopped dates are cherished companions to fruit-infused scones.

Rehydrating Dried Fruits

To ensure plump and flavorful dried fruits in your scones, consider rehydrating them before mixing. A brief soak in warm water or fruit juice revives their texture and taste. Drain and pat the rehydrated fruits dry before incorporating them into the dough. This approach prevents the dried fruits from absorbing too much moisture from the dough during baking.

Balancing Sweetness and Tartness

The harmony between sweetness and tartness defines the allure of fruit-infused scones. Natural sugars in the fruits provide inherent sweetness, which can be accentuated by adding a touch of granulated sugar to the dough. Achieving the ideal equilibrium involves adjusting the ratio of sweet to tart fruits, allowing you to tailor the scones to your palate.

When working with tart fruits—like cranberries or sour cherries—consider introducing citrus zest or a simple glaze. A citrus-infused glaze, crafted from fresh juice and powdered sugar, imparts an additional layer of flavor that beautifully contrasts with the fruit's tartness.

Heavenly fruit-infused scones are a testament to the beauty of merging fresh and dried fruits with the art of scone baking. These scones capture the essence of each season, offering a symphony of flavors that dance across your taste buds. By embracing the delicate balance between sweetness and tartness, you can craft scones that epitomize the pure joy of nature's bounty.

Chapter 4: Decadent Chocolate Scones

Decadent chocolate scones offer an irresistible fusion of rich chocolate and the classic scone, resulting in a treat that's as luxurious as it is comforting.

Cocoa vs. Chocolate Chips

Cocoa Powder

Ingredients:

- 2 cups all-purpose flour
- 1/3 cup unsweetened cocoa powder (natural or Dutch-processed)
- 1/4 cup granulated sugar
- 1 tablespoon baking powder
- 1/2 teaspoon salt
- 1/2 cup unsalted butter, cold and cubed
- 3/4 cup milk or cream
- 1 teaspoon vanilla extract

Instructions:

1. Preheat your oven to 400°F (200°C) and line a baking sheet with parchment paper.
2. In a large mixing bowl, whisk together the flour, cocoa powder, sugar, baking powder, and salt.
3. Add the cold, cubed butter to the dry ingredients. Use a pastry cutter or your fingertips to work the butter into the flour until the mixture resembles coarse crumbs.
4. Pour in the milk or cream and vanilla extract. Mix gently until the dough just comes together. Be careful not to overmix.
5. Turn the dough out onto a lightly floured surface. Pat it into a circle about 1 inch thick.

6. Cut the dough into wedges or rounds using a round biscuit cutter. Place the scones on the prepared baking sheet.
7. Bake for 15-18 minutes or until the scones are firm to the touch and the tops are slightly cracked.
8. Allow the scones to cool slightly before serving.

Chocolate Chip Scones
Ingredients:

- 2 cups all-purpose flour
- 1/4 cup granulated sugar
- 1 tablespoon baking powder
- 1/2 teaspoon salt
- 1/2 cup unsalted butter, cold and cubed
- 1/2 cup chocolate chips (semisweet, bittersweet, or white chocolate)
- 3/4 cup milk or cream
- 1 teaspoon vanilla extract

Instructions:

1. Preheat your oven to 400°F (200°C) and line a baking sheet with parchment paper.
2. In a large mixing bowl, whisk together the flour, sugar, baking powder, and salt.
3. Add the cold, cubed butter to the dry ingredients. Use a pastry cutter or your fingertips to work the butter into the flour until the mixture resembles coarse crumbs.
4. Stir in the chocolate chips.
5. Pour in the milk or cream and vanilla extract. Mix gently until the dough just comes together. Be careful not to overmix.
6. Turn the dough out onto a lightly floured surface. Pat it into a circle about 1 inch thick.
7. Cut the dough into wedges or rounds using a round biscuit cutter. Place the scones on the prepared baking sheet.
8. Bake for 15-18 minutes or until the scones are firm to the touch and golden brown.
9. Allow the scones to cool slightly before serving.

Variations and Enhancements

Fruit and Chocolate Harmony

For cocoa-infused scones, consider adding 1/2 cup of dried cranberries or cherries to the dough for a burst of tart sweetness.

Nuts for Texture

For chocolate chip scones, incorporate 1/2 cup of chopped toasted walnuts or pecans to introduce a satisfying crunch and nutty flavor.

Decadent chocolate scones offer a harmonious union of traditional scone goodness and the exquisite allure of chocolate. By incorporating cocoa or chocolate chips and experimenting with complementary flavors, you can create scones that are the epitome of indulgence. These scones are a treat to the senses, inviting you to savor the symphony of flavors in each delectable bite.

Chapter 5: Savory Herb and Cheese Scones

Herb-Infused Scone Varieties

Savory herb and cheese scones add a sophisticated twist to the traditional scone, offering a delectable blend of aromatic herbs and rich cheeses that create a savory sensation.

Choosing the Right Herbs

The selection of herbs is crucial in creating scones that burst with flavor. Opt for fresh herbs like rosemary, thyme, chives, parsley, or even a combination of these. The earthy and fragrant notes of these herbs infuse the scones with a depth of taste that's both comforting and invigorating.

Incorporating Herbs into the Dough

To ensure an even distribution of herbs, finely chop them before incorporating them into the dry ingredients. As you work the cold, cubed butter into the flour mixture, the herbs will disperse throughout the dough, creating a harmonious infusion of flavor.

Choosing the Right Cheeses

The choice of cheese is pivotal in achieving scones that are rich in both texture and taste. Consider cheeses that possess robust flavors and complement the herbs. Sharp cheddar, Gruyère, Parmesan, feta, or a blend of two cheeses can elevate the scone's character.

Balancing Herbs and Cheese

Achieving the perfect balance between herbs and cheese requires a keen palate. Start conservatively by adding a modest amount of herbs and cheese to the dough. As you mix the ingredients, taste and adjust accordingly. The goal is to create a symphony of flavors where the herbs and cheese enhance one another without overpowering.

Pairing with Soups and Salads
Savory Scone Companions
Savory herb and cheese scones make for exceptional companions to soups and salads. The scones' hearty texture and nuanced flavors amplify the dining experience, transforming a simple meal into a culinary delight.
Scone Selection for Salads
When pairing scones with salads, consider the scone's herb and cheese combination. Scones infused with mild herbs like chives and parsley offer versatility, harmonizing with a variety of salads—from light and refreshing greens to substantial pasta and grain-based salads.

Instructions for Herb and Cheese Scones
Ingredients:

- 2 cups all-purpose flour
- 1 tablespoon baking powder
- 1/2 teaspoon salt
- 1/2 cup unsalted butter, cold and cubed
- 1/2 cup grated sharp cheddar cheese
- 2 tablespoons finely chopped fresh herbs (rosemary, thyme, chives, etc.)
- 3/4 cup milk or cream

Instructions:

1. Preheat your oven to 400°F (200°C) and line a baking sheet with parchment paper.
2. In a large mixing bowl, whisk together the flour, baking powder, and salt.
3. Add the cold, cubed butter to the dry ingredients. Use a pastry cutter or your fingertips to work the butter into the flour until the mixture resembles coarse crumbs.

4. Stir in the grated cheddar cheese and chopped fresh herbs.
5. Pour in the milk or cream and gently mix until the dough just comes together. Be cautious not to overmix.
6. Turn the dough out onto a lightly floured surface. Pat it into a circle about 1 inch thick.
7. Cut the dough into wedges or rounds using a round biscuit cutter. Place the scones on the prepared baking sheet.
8. Bake for 15-18 minutes or until the scones are firm to the touch and golden brown.
9. Allow the scones to cool slightly before serving.

Savory herb and cheese scones provide an avenue for savoring the robust flavors of fresh herbs and rich cheeses in a single bite. With a careful selection of herbs and cheeses, you can create scones that harmonize beautifully with soups, salads, or simply enjoyed on their own. These scones invite you to explore the savory side of scone baking and relish in their intricate taste profiles.

Chapter 6: Wholesome Whole Grain Scones

Healthier Scone Alternatives

Wholesome whole grain scones provide a nutritious twist on the classic treat, offering a more health-conscious option without compromising on flavor and satisfaction.

Whole Grain Flour Substitutes

Embracing whole grains introduces a spectrum of flavors and textures to scones. Whole wheat flour, oat flour, spelt flour, and even almond flour can replace some or all of the all-purpose flour in your scone recipes. These alternatives contribute a heartier taste and an increased nutrient profile.

Balancing Health and Flavor

While whole grains add nutritional value, they can alter the scone's texture and flavor. Achieving the perfect balance between health and taste requires experimentation and a touch of creativity. A blend of whole grain and all-purpose flours can yield scones that are both nutritious and delightful.

Whole Wheat, Oats, and More
Whole Wheat Flour Scones
Ingredients:

- 1 1/2 cups whole wheat flour
- 1/2 cup all-purpose flour
- 1/4 cup granulated sugar
- 1 tablespoon baking powder
- 1/2 teaspoon salt
- 1/2 cup unsalted butter, cold and cubed
- 3/4 cup milk or buttermilk
- 1 teaspoon vanilla extract

Instructions:

1. Preheat your oven to 400°F (200°C) and line a baking sheet with parchment paper.
2. In a mixing bowl, combine the whole wheat flour, all-purpose flour, sugar, baking powder, and salt.
3. Add the cold, cubed butter to the dry ingredients. Use a pastry cutter or your fingertips to work the butter into the flour until the mixture resembles coarse crumbs.
4. Pour in the milk or buttermilk and vanilla extract. Mix gently until the dough just comes together. Be cautious not to overmix.
5. Turn the dough out onto a lightly floured surface. Pat it into a circle about 1 inch thick.
6. Cut the dough into wedges or rounds using a round biscuit cutter. Place the scones on the prepared baking sheet.
7. Bake for 15-18 minutes or until the scones are firm to the touch and golden brown.
8. Allow the scones to cool slightly before serving.

Nutritional Benefits and Flavor Combinations

Nutritional Highlights

Whole grain scones offer a range of nutritional benefits, including increased fiber content, vitamins, and minerals. The presence of whole grains contributes to better digestion, sustained energy, and overall well-being.

Flavor Combinations

Whole grain scones invite creative pairings of flavors. Consider adding dried fruits, nuts, or seeds to enhance both the taste and nutritional value. Chopped dried apricots, toasted almonds, or chia seeds can elevate your whole grain scones to new heights.

Wholesome whole grain scones invite a wholesome approach to scone baking, combining the nourishing power of whole grains with the comfort of a classic treat. Whether experimenting with different whole grain flours or adding nutrient-rich mix-ins, you can create scones that cater to both your taste buds and your health-conscious desires.

Chapter 7: Gluten-Free Delights: Scones for Everyone

Gluten-Free Flours and Binders

Creating gluten-free scones opens a world of possibilities for individuals with dietary restrictions. By exploring alternative flours and binders, you can craft scones that are both delectable and suitable for a gluten-free lifestyle.

Alternative Flour Options

Embracing gluten-free flours is the cornerstone of successful gluten-free baking. Consider using almond flour, rice flour, oat flour, tapioca flour, or a blend of these options. Mixing different flours can yield a balanced texture and flavor, enhancing the scone's overall appeal.

Binding Agents for Gluten-Free Baking

Gluten, a protein found in wheat, provides structure to baked goods. In gluten-free baking, incorporating binding agents is essential to achieve the desired crumb and texture. Xanthan gum and psyllium husk powder are common binding agents that help mimic the elasticity of gluten.

Texture Enhancement Techniques

Texture Challenges in Gluten-Free Baking

Crafting gluten-free scones with an optimal texture can be challenging due to the absence of gluten's binding properties. Employing the right techniques can result in scones that are tender, moist, and reminiscent of traditional counterparts.

Increasing Moisture

Gluten-free flours tend to absorb more moisture than wheat flour. To counter potential dryness, consider adding a bit more liquid to the recipe. This adjustment can help maintain a pleasantly moist texture.

Balancing Dry Ingredients

Maintaining the correct balance of dry to wet ingredients is crucial. This balance impacts the scone's structure and helps prevent a gritty or crumbly texture.

Flavorful Gluten-Free Mix-Ins

Exploring Mix-In Possibilities

Elevating gluten-free scones involves experimenting with mix-ins that enhance both taste and texture. Incorporating mix-ins like dried fruits, nuts, seeds, or even chocolate chips can transform your gluten-free scones into delightful creations.

Dried Fruits and Nuts

Adding dried fruits such as raisins, cranberries, or apricots introduces bursts of flavor and a pleasant chewiness. Chopped nuts, like almonds, pecans, or walnuts, contribute not only crunch but also depth to the scone's character.

Chocolate Indulgences

For a touch of decadence, consider integrating chocolate chips or cocoa nibs into your gluten-free scones. The richness of cocoa or chocolate complements the scone's texture, resulting in a gluten-free treat that appeals to all palates.

Gluten-free scones offer a realm of flavorful possibilities for individuals with dietary limitations. By exploring a diverse range of alternative flours, mastering the use of binding agents, and honing texture techniques, you can create scones that satisfy both taste and dietary needs. Infuse creativity into your baking by adding delightful mix-ins, ensuring that gluten-free scone lovers can also indulge in the delights of scone baking.

Chapter 8: Breakfast Bliss: Scone Sandwiches and Accompaniments

Crafting Scone Breakfast Sandwiches

Elevate your breakfast experience with scone sandwiches, where the hearty texture of scones meets an array of delicious fillings. From savory to sweet, these scone sandwiches are versatile and satisfying.

Savory Scone Breakfast Sandwich

Ingredients:

- 1 savory cheese and herb scone (from Chapter 5)
- 2 slices cooked bacon
- 1 scrambled egg
- Sliced tomato
- Baby spinach leaves
- Salt and pepper to taste

Instructions:

1. Slice the savory cheese and herb scone in half.
2. Layer one half with cooked bacon, scrambled egg, sliced tomato, and baby spinach leaves.
3. Season with salt and pepper to taste.
4. Place the other half of the scone on top to form a sandwich.
5. Enjoy your savory scone breakfast sandwich!

Delicious Spreads and Toppings

Enhance your scone experience with an array of spreads and toppings that complement their flavors and textures.

Sweet Cream Cheese Spread

Ingredients:

- 4 oz cream cheese, softened

- 2 tablespoons honey
- 1 teaspoon vanilla extract

Instructions:

1. In a bowl, combine softened cream cheese, honey, and vanilla extract.
2. Mix until smooth and well blended.
3. Spread the sweet cream cheese on a plain or fruit-infused scone.

Lemon Curd and Fresh Berries
Ingredients:

- 1 batch of lemon curd (store-bought or homemade)
- Fresh mixed berries (strawberries, blueberries, raspberries)

Instructions:

1. Spread a layer of lemon curd on a plain or citrus-flavored scone.
2. Top with an assortment of fresh mixed berries for a burst of sweetness and color.

Coffee and Tea Pairings

Pairing your scone creations with the right coffee or tea can elevate your breakfast or afternoon tea experience.

Classic Earl Grey Tea

Pair with: Classic Plain Scones

Notes: The citrusy notes of Earl Grey tea complement the buttery flavors of plain scones, creating a harmonious balance.

Rich Espresso or Coffee

Pair with: Decadent Chocolate Scones

Notes: The bold richness of coffee enhances the indulgence of chocolate scones, making for a satisfying combination.

Herbal Chamomile Tea

Pair with: Wholesome Whole Grain Scones

Notes: The gentle flavors of chamomile tea accentuate the earthy undertones of whole grain scones, creating a soothing ensemble.

Breakfast bliss awaits with scone sandwiches and accompaniments. Whether you're indulging in a savory breakfast sandwich, exploring sweet spreads, or pairing scones with your favorite coffee or tea, these delightful combinations are bound to make your mornings and afternoons truly memorable.

Chapter 9: Elegant Afternoon Tea Scones

Delicate Scones for Tea Time

Elevate your afternoon tea experience with elegant scones that are designed to perfectly accompany a cup of tea. Delicate in both appearance and flavor, these scones add an air of sophistication to your tea table

Choosing Delicate Flavors

When crafting scones for afternoon tea, opt for delicate and refined flavors. Think lavender-infused, lemon-poppyseed, or vanilla-rose. These flavors provide a subtle yet captivating enhancement to the tea experience.

Serving with Clotted Cream and Jam

The Quintessential Pairing

Serving scones with clotted cream and jam is a tradition that dates back generations. The interplay of rich, creamy clotted cream and the sweetness of jam creates a harmonious balance that elevates the scone's flavor profile.

Homemade Clotted Cream
Ingredients:

- 1 cup heavy cream

Instructions:

1. Pour the heavy cream into a wide, shallow dish.
2. Bake in the oven at 180°F (82°C) for about 12 hours or until a thick layer forms on the surface.
3. Remove from the oven and let cool. Refrigerate until ready to serve.

Setting the Perfect Tea Table

Creating an Atmosphere

Afternoon tea is as much about ambiance as it is about the treats. Set the stage for an elegant tea experience by paying attention to the details.

Table Decor

Adorn your tea table with a lace tablecloth, delicate china tea cups, and vintage tea pots. Fresh flowers in a vase and dainty napkins add a touch of charm.

Tea Selection

Offer a variety of tea options to cater to different preferences. Classic choices like Earl Grey, Darjeeling, and herbal blends like chamomile or lavender can cater to diverse tastes.

Arranging the Scones

Present the scones on tiered cake stands, allowing guests to easily access the delicacies while adding to the visual allure of the tea table.

Elegant afternoon tea scones offer a refined touch to your tea time gatherings. With delicate flavors, the classic pairing of clotted cream and jam, and careful attention to table setting, you can create an atmosphere that transports you and your guests to a world of elegance and indulgence.

Chapter 10: Scone-Inspired Desserts

Turning Scones into Sweet Treats

Unleash the versatility of scones by transforming them into delightful and creative desserts. With a touch of innovation, scones can be the foundation for a range of sweet and indulgent treats.

Scone Crusts for Pies and Tarts

A Sweet Base

The crumbly texture and buttery flavor of scones make them a fantastic base for pies and tarts. Using scones as a crust introduces a unique twist that complements various fillings.

Berry Scone Tart
Ingredients:

- 1 batch of berry-infused scone dough (from Chapter 3)
- 2 cups mixed fresh berries (strawberries, blueberries, raspberries)
- 1/4 cup granulated sugar
- 1 tablespoon cornstarch

Instructions:

1. Preheat your oven to 375°F (190°C) and grease a tart pan.
2. Press the berry-infused scone dough evenly into the tart pan to create the crust.
3. In a bowl, toss the mixed berries with granulated sugar and cornstarch.
4. Spread the berry mixture over the scone crust.
5. Bake for 25-30 minutes or until the crust is golden and the berries are bubbling.
6. Allow to cool before slicing and serving.

Transformative Dessert Recipes
Scone Bread Pudding
Ingredients:

- 6-8 stale scones, cubed (plain or flavored)
- 2 cups milk
- 3/4 cup granulated sugar
- 4 large eggs
- 1 teaspoon vanilla extract
- 1/2 teaspoon cinnamon
- 1/4 teaspoon nutmeg
- 1/2 cup raisins or chocolate chips (optional)

Instructions:

1. Preheat your oven to 350°F (175°C) and grease a baking dish.
2. Place the cubed scones in the baking dish.
3. In a bowl, whisk together milk, sugar, eggs, vanilla extract, cinnamon, and nutmeg.
4. Pour the milk mixture over the scones, ensuring they're well soaked.
5. If using, sprinkle raisins or chocolate chips over the top.
6. Bake for 40-45 minutes or until the pudding is set and golden on top.
7. Let cool slightly before serving. Serve warm with a drizzle of caramel sauce or a scoop of vanilla ice cream.

Scone-inspired desserts unlock a world of creativity in the kitchen. Whether you're crafting scone crusts for pies and tarts or reimagining scones into bread pudding, these transformative dessert recipes showcase the endless possibilities of scone-based sweets.

Chapter 11: Vegan and Dairy-Free Scone Creations

Dairy Alternatives for Scone Making

Explore the world of vegan and dairy-free scone baking, where plant-based ingredients create scones that are both compassionate and delicious. With the right substitutions, you can achieve the same beloved scone texture and flavor.

Choosing Dairy Alternatives

Replace dairy butter with plant-based alternatives like coconut oil, vegan margarine, or non-dairy buttery spreads. These options lend a richness and moisture to your scones, ensuring they're just as delectable as their dairy counterparts.

Egg Replacements and Binding Agents

Flaxseed "Eggs"

For each "egg," combine 1 tablespoon ground flaxseed with 3 tablespoons water. Let it sit for a few minutes until it thickens, forming an egg-like consistency.

Applesauce

Swap each egg with 1/4 cup unsweetened applesauce to provide moisture and binding properties.

Plant-Based Yogurt

Use plant-based yogurt as an egg replacement. It adds moisture and a touch of tanginess to the scones.

Plant-Based Flavors and Fillings

Coconut and Pineapple Scones

Ingredients:

- 2 cups all-purpose flour
- 1/4 cup granulated sugar
- 1 tablespoon baking powder
- 1/2 teaspoon salt

- 1/2 cup coconut oil, solid
- 1/2 cup canned coconut milk (full fat)
- 1 teaspoon vanilla extract
- 1/2 cup diced pineapple (fresh or canned)
- 1/4 cup shredded coconut (unsweetened)

Instructions:

1. Preheat your oven to 400°F (200°C) and line a baking sheet with parchment paper.
2. In a mixing bowl, whisk together the flour, sugar, baking powder, and salt.
3. Add the solid coconut oil and use your fingers to work it into the dry ingredients until crumbly.
4. Stir in the canned coconut milk and vanilla extract until a dough forms.
5. Gently fold in the diced pineapple and shredded coconut.
6. Turn the dough out onto a lightly floured surface and shape it into a circle. Cut into wedges.
7. Place the scones on the prepared baking sheet and bake for 15-18 minutes, or until golden.
8. Allow to cool before serving.

Vegan and dairy-free scone creations provide a compassionate twist on the classic treat. With dairy alternatives, egg replacements, and a range of plant-based flavors and fillings, you can bake scones that cater to a variety of dietary preferences while maintaining the beloved scone texture and taste.

Chapter 12: International Flavors: Spicing Up Your Scones

Exploring Global Scone Variations

Embark on a flavorful journey by infusing your scone recipes with international influences. From exotic ingredients to traditional preparation methods, international scone variations offer a taste of culinary diversity.

Incorporating Spices and Herbs

Masala Chai Scones

Ingredients:

- 2 cups all-purpose flour
- 1/4 cup granulated sugar
- 1 tablespoon baking powder
- 1/2 teaspoon salt
- 1 teaspoon ground cinnamon
- 1/2 teaspoon ground cardamom
- 1/4 teaspoon ground ginger
- 1/4 teaspoon ground cloves
- 1/4 teaspoon ground nutmeg
- 1/2 cup cold unsalted butter, cubed
- 3/4 cup milk (dairy or plant-based)
- 1 teaspoon vanilla extract

Instructions:

1. Preheat your oven to 400°F (200°C) and line a baking sheet with parchment paper.
2. In a mixing bowl, whisk together the flour, sugar, baking powder, salt, and spices.

3. Add the cold, cubed butter and use a pastry cutter or your fingers to work it into the dry ingredients until the mixture resembles coarse crumbs.
4. Pour in the milk and vanilla extract. Mix gently until the dough forms.
5. Turn the dough out onto a floured surface, shape into a circle, and cut into wedges.
6. Place the scones on the baking sheet and bake for 15-18 minutes, or until golden.
7. Let cool before serving.

Infusing Cultural Influences
Matcha Green Tea Scones
Ingredients:

- 2 cups all-purpose flour
- 1/4 cup granulated sugar
- 1 tablespoon matcha green tea powder
- 1 tablespoon baking powder
- 1/2 teaspoon salt
- 1/2 cup cold unsalted butter, cubed
- 3/4 cup milk (dairy or plant-based)
- 1 teaspoon vanilla extract

Instructions:

1. Preheat your oven to 400°F (200°C) and line a baking sheet with parchment paper.
2. In a mixing bowl, whisk together the flour, sugar, matcha powder, baking powder, and salt.
3. Add the cold, cubed butter and work it into the dry ingredients until the mixture resembles coarse crumbs.
4. Pour in the milk and vanilla extract. Mix gently until the dough forms.
5. Turn the dough out onto a floured surface, shape into a circle, and cut into wedges.
6. Place the scones on the baking sheet and bake for 15-18 minutes, or until golden.
7. Let cool before serving.

International flavors introduce a new dimension to the world of scone baking. By incorporating spices, herbs, and cultural influences from around the globe, you can create scones that transport your taste buds to far-off lands, showcasing the beauty of culinary diversity.

Chapter 13: Nutty Indulgences: Nut-Flavored Scone Varieties

Elevating Scones with Nuts

Discover the delightful world of nut-flavored scones, where the rich and distinctive flavors of various nuts take center stage. From subtle hints to bold nutty profiles, these scone varieties add an indulgent twist to your baking repertoire.

Nut Butters, Chunks, and Powders

Hazelnut and Chocolate Chunk Scones

Ingredients:

- 2 cups all-purpose flour
- 1/4 cup granulated sugar
- 1 tablespoon baking powder
- 1/2 teaspoon salt
- 1/2 cup cold unsalted butter, cubed
- 1/2 cup chopped hazelnuts
- 1/2 cup chocolate chunks or chips
- 3/4 cup milk (dairy or plant-based)
- 1 teaspoon vanilla extract

Instructions:

1. Preheat your oven to 400°F (200°C) and line a baking sheet with parchment paper.
2. In a mixing bowl, whisk together the flour, sugar, baking powder, and salt.
3. Add the cold, cubed butter and work it into the dry ingredients until the mixture resembles coarse crumbs.
4. Stir in the chopped hazelnuts and chocolate chunks.

5. Pour in the milk and vanilla extract. Mix gently until the dough forms.

6. Turn the dough out onto a floured surface, shape into a circle, and cut into wedges.

7. Place the scones on the baking sheet and bake for 15-18 minutes, or until golden.

8. Let cool before serving.

Balancing Nutty Textures and Flavors
Almond and Apricot Scones
Ingredients:

- 2 cups all-purpose flour
- 1/4 cup granulated sugar
- 1 tablespoon baking powder
- 1/2 teaspoon salt
- 1/2 cup cold unsalted butter, cubed
- 1/2 cup chopped almonds
- 1/2 cup chopped dried apricots
- 3/4 cup milk (dairy or plant-based)
- 1 teaspoon almond extract

Instructions:

1. Preheat your oven to 400°F (200°C) and line a baking sheet with parchment paper.
2. In a mixing bowl, whisk together the flour, sugar, baking powder, and salt.
3. Add the cold, cubed butter and work it into the dry ingredients until the mixture resembles coarse crumbs.
4. Stir in the chopped almonds and dried apricots.
5. Pour in the milk and almond extract. Mix gently until the dough forms.
6. Turn the dough out onto a floured surface, shape into a circle, and cut into wedges.
7. Place the scones on the baking sheet and bake for 15-18 minutes, or until golden.
8. Let cool before serving.

Nut-flavored scone varieties offer a nutty twist to your scone repertoire. With the incorporation of various nut elements, including nut butters, chunks, and powders, you can create scones that celebrate the distinct flavors and textures of different nuts, resulting in indulgent and satisfying treats.

Chapter 14: Filling and Fulfilling: Scones with Fillings

Filling Scones with Sweet and Savory Goodness

Take your scone creations to the next level by incorporating delicious fillings that add an extra layer of flavor and excitement. Whether sweet or savory, filled scones are sure to delight your taste buds.

Techniques for Encasing Fillings

Folded Pockets

Create pockets in the scone dough and fold it over the filling. Seal the edges to prevent leaks during baking.

Double Layered

Place a layer of dough, add the filling, and cover with another layer of dough. Press the edges to seal, creating a sandwich-like scone.

Stuffed Scones

Roll out the dough into rounds, place the filling on one half, and fold the other half over the filling. Press the edges to seal.

Creative Filling Combinations

Savory Spinach and Feta Stuffed Scones

Ingredients:

- 2 cups all-purpose flour
- 1 tablespoon baking powder
- 1/2 teaspoon salt
- 1/2 cup cold unsalted butter, cubed
- 1/2 cup milk (dairy or plant-based)
- 1 cup fresh spinach, cooked and chopped
- 1/2 cup crumbled feta cheese
- 1/4 cup finely chopped onion
- 1 clove garlic, minced
- Salt and pepper to taste

Instructions:

1. Preheat your oven to 400°F (200°C) and line a baking sheet with parchment paper.
2. In a mixing bowl, whisk together the flour, baking powder, and salt.
3. Add the cold, cubed butter and work it into the dry ingredients until the mixture resembles coarse crumbs.
4. Pour in the milk and mix gently until the dough forms.
5. In a separate bowl, combine cooked chopped spinach, crumbled feta, chopped onion, minced garlic, salt, and pepper.
6. Roll out portions of the dough into rounds. Place a spoonful of the spinach and feta mixture on one half, then fold the other half over the filling. Press the edges to seal.
7. Place the stuffed scones on the baking sheet and bake for 15-18 minutes, or until golden.
8. Let cool slightly before serving.

Sweet Raspberry Jam-Filled Scones
Ingredients:

- 2 cups all-purpose flour
- 1/4 cup granulated sugar
- 1 tablespoon baking powder
- 1/2 teaspoon salt
- 1/2 cup cold unsalted butter, cubed
- 1/2 cup milk (dairy or plant-based)
- Raspberry jam

Instructions:

1. Preheat your oven to 400°F (200°C) and line a baking sheet with parchment paper.
2. In a mixing bowl, whisk together the flour, sugar, baking

powder, and salt.

3. Add the cold, cubed butter and work it into the dry ingredients until the mixture resembles coarse crumbs.
4. Pour in the milk and mix gently until the dough forms.
5. Roll out portions of the dough into rounds. Place a spoonful of raspberry jam in the center, then fold the dough over the jam. Press the edges to seal.
6. Place the filled scones on the baking sheet and bake for 15-18 minutes, or until golden.
7. Let cool slightly before serving.

Filling scones with a variety of sweet and savory fillings opens up endless possibilities for flavor combinations. Whether you're experimenting with folded pockets, double-layered scones, or stuffed creations, these techniques allow you to craft scones that are not only visually appealing but also bursting with mouthwatering goodness.

Chapter 15: Butter, Cream, and Other Secrets: Scone Essentials

Exploring Different Fat Choices

Dive into the world of scone essentials, where the choice of fats can transform the texture, flavor, and overall experience of your scones. From classic butter to innovative alternatives, understanding the role of fats is key to mastering the art of scone baking.

The Role of Cream in Scones

Clotted Cream and Scones: A Match Made in Heaven

Clotted cream is a luxurious addition to scones that enhances their flavor and texture. This thick, silky cream lends a rich and velvety element that perfectly complements the crumbly and slightly sweet nature of scones.

Making Your Own Clotted Cream
Ingredients:

- 2 cups heavy cream

Instructions:

1. Preheat your oven to 180°F (82°C).
2. Pour the heavy cream into a shallow, ovenproof dish.
3. Place the dish in the oven and let it bake for 12-14 hours until a thick layer forms on top.
4. Remove from the oven and let cool. Refrigerate before serving.

Butter and Beyond: Innovative Ingredients
Greek Yogurt Scones
Ingredients:

- 2 cups all-purpose flour
- 1/4 cup granulated sugar
- 1 tablespoon baking powder
- 1/2 teaspoon salt
- 1/2 cup cold unsalted butter, cubed
- 1/2 cup Greek yogurt
- 1/4 cup milk (dairy or plant-based)
- 1 teaspoon vanilla extract

Instructions:

1. Preheat your oven to 400°F (200°C) and line a baking sheet with parchment paper.
2. In a mixing bowl, whisk together the flour, sugar, baking powder, and salt.
3. Add the cold, cubed butter and work it into the dry ingredients until the mixture resembles coarse crumbs.
4. In a separate bowl, combine Greek yogurt, milk, and vanilla extract. Mix until smooth.
5. Pour the wet mixture into the dry mixture and gently combine until the dough forms.
6. Turn the dough out onto a floured surface, shape into a circle, and cut into wedges.
7. Place the scones on the baking sheet and bake for 15-18 minutes, or until golden.
8. Let cool before serving.

Mastering the essentials of scone baking involves understanding the role of fats, exploring the magic of clotted cream, and experimenting with innovative ingredients. Whether you're opting for classic butter, exploring the decadence of clotted cream, or venturing into unique creations like Greek yogurt scones, these secrets add depth and complexity to your scone journey.

Chapter 16: Mini Scones, Maximum Flavor

Bite-Sized Scone Delights

Embrace the joy of bite-sized scone delights with these miniature versions that pack a punch of flavor in every bite. Mini scones are not only adorable but also allow you to explore an array of tastes without committing to a full-sized treat.

Perfecting Miniature Scone Texture

Balance in Small Packages

Creating mini scones requires attention to detail to ensure they maintain the classic scone texture. To perfect these miniature treats, follow these key steps:

Cold Ingredients: Just like with regular-sized scones, use cold butter and milk. Cold ingredients help create the sought-after flakiness.

Gentle Mixing: Handle the dough gently to avoid overworking it, as this could lead to tough mini scones.

Uniformity: Ensure that the scone dough is of consistent thickness when rolling or shaping it. This helps in achieving even baking.

Serving Mini Scones at Gatherings

Mini Scone Tasting Platter

Create an impressive and diverse mini scone tasting platter for your gatherings. This arrangement allows your guests to explore a range of flavors in a delightful assortment.

Flavor Variety

Offer an assortment of flavors that cater to various tastes:

Classic Plain: A timeless choice for scone aficionados.

Fruit-Infused: Explore mini scones with bursts of fresh fruits or dried fruits.

Chocolate Delights: Indulge in mini chocolate chip or cocoa scones.

Savory Creations: Present mini herb and cheese or other savory scone varieties.

Global Inspirations: Introduce international flavors with mini scones featuring unique spices and ingredients.

Accompaniments

Enhance the mini scone experience by providing an array of accompaniments:

Clotted Cream: The luxurious addition that pairs wonderfully with both sweet and savory mini scones.

Jam and Spreads: Offer a selection of jams, fruit preserves, and spreads that complement the various flavors.

Honey and Butter: Provide honey for a touch of natural sweetness and butter for a classic pairing.

Presentation

Elevate the visual appeal of your mini scone platter with these presentation tips:

Decorative Platter: Arrange the mini scones on an elegant platter or a tiered stand for a sophisticated touch.

Place Cards: Label each flavor with small place cards, adding a charming and informative element.

Mini scones bring a new dimension of delight to your gatherings, allowing everyone to sample an assortment of flavors. By mastering the art of mini scone texture, offering diverse flavor choices, and presenting them with flair, you're sure to impress your guests with a charming and flavorful mini scone experience.

Chapter 17: Whipped Cream and Homemade Jams: Perfect Scone Pairings

Crafting Whipped Cream Toppings

Discover the art of creating luscious whipped cream toppings that elevate your scone experience to new heights. The creamy, dreamy texture of whipped cream adds a luxurious touch that complements the crumbly scone perfectly.

Homemade Jams, Preserves, and Curds

Classic Strawberry Jam
Ingredients:

- 2 cups fresh strawberries, hulled and diced
- 1 cup granulated sugar
- 2 tablespoons lemon juice

Instructions:

1. In a saucepan, combine diced strawberries, sugar, and lemon juice.
2. Cook over medium heat, stirring occasionally, until the mixture thickens and reaches a jam-like consistency.
3. Remove from heat and let cool. Transfer to sterilized jars and store in the refrigerator.

Lemon Curd
Ingredients:

- 3 large eggs
- 3/4 cup granulated sugar
- 1/2 cup fresh lemon juice

- Zest of 2 lemons
- 1/4 cup unsalted butter, cubed

Instructions:

1. In a saucepan, whisk together eggs, sugar, lemon juice, and lemon zest.
2. Cook over low heat, stirring constantly, until the mixture thickens and coats the back of a spoon.
3. Remove from heat and whisk in the cubed butter until melted and smooth.
4. Strain the curd through a fine mesh sieve into a bowl. Let cool before transferring to a jar. Store in the refrigerator.

Elevating Scone Flavors with Pairings
Scone and Whipped Cream Pairings

Classic Plain Scone + Vanilla Whipped Cream: The ultimate pairing of rich vanilla cream and the simple elegance of a plain scone.

Chocolate Scone + Espresso Whipped Cream: A decadent duo that marries the flavors of chocolate and coffee with the smoothness of whipped cream.

Scone and Homemade Jam Pairings

Fruit-Infused Scone + Berry Jam: Enhance the fruity flavors of your scone with a burst of vibrant berry jam.

Savory Scone + Tomato Jam: A surprising savory pairing that complements the scone's herbs and cheese with the tangy sweetness of tomato jam.

Scone and Curd Pairings

Lemon Scone + Lemon Curd: A zesty delight that brings the bright flavors of lemon to the forefront.

Vanilla-Rose Scone + Raspberry Curd: Elevate your scone with the delicate floral notes of vanilla-rose and the sweet-tartness of raspberry curd.

The art of scone pairings lies in creating luxurious whipped cream toppings and crafting homemade jams, preserves, and curds that enhance the scone's flavors. From classic combinations to innovative pairings, these elements add an extra layer of indulgence to your scone experience.

Chapter 18: Scones for Special Celebrations

Customizing Scones for Occasions

Create a lasting impression by tailoring your scones to the theme and tone of your special celebrations. Whether it's a milestone birthday, a bridal shower, a holiday gathering, or any other joyous event, customizing scones adds a delightful touch that makes the occasion even more memorable.

Themed Decoration and Presentation

Birthday Bash Scones

Craft scones that mirror the birthday person's favorite flavors and colors. Transform plain scones into mini masterpieces by decorating them with icing, colorful sprinkles, and edible decorations that reflect the celebratory spirit.

Holiday Scone Extravaganza

Embrace the essence of holidays with themed scone creations:

Christmas Delights: Shape scone dough into festive symbols like Christmas trees, stars, or snowflakes. Infuse the scones with seasonal spices and adorn them with a dusting of powdered sugar for a snowy touch.

Halloween Treats: Create pumpkin-shaped scones and incorporate pumpkin puree into the dough for a warm autumn flavor. Add a touch of cinnamon and nutmeg for that quintessential fall taste.

Valentine's Love: Craft heart-shaped scones that capture the spirit of love. Incorporate raspberry or strawberry flavors and drizzle them with a sweet glaze for an extra romantic touch.

Bridal Shower Elegance

Capture the elegance of a bridal shower with refined scone selections:

Delicate Flavors: opt for scone flavors that match the bride's preferences, such as lavender-infused, vanilla-rose, or white chocolate and raspberry.

Elegant Decorations: Decorate the scones with pastel-colored icing, edible flowers, or delicate drizzles for an air of sophistication.

Floral Accents: Integrate edible floral elements like candied rose petals or lavender buds to bring a touch of romance and beauty to the spread.

Memorable Scone-Centric Events

Scone Tasting Party

Host an enchanting scone tasting party where guests can embark on a flavor adventure:

Scone Selection: Provide an array of scone flavors, ranging from classic to innovative, allowing guests to explore different taste profiles.

Pairing Possibilities: Offer a selection of whipped creams, jams, curds, and spreads for guests to pair with their scones. Create tasting cards that suggest unique combinations.

Scone-Making Workshop

Turn your celebration into a hands-on experience with a scone-making workshop:

Interactive Experience: Set up stations with various scone ingredients and fillings, inviting participants to experiment and create their own scone masterpieces.

Guided Instruction: Provide step-by-step guidance on scone making, from mixing the dough to shaping and baking.

Personalized Creations: Let attendees customize their scones with an array of ingredients, encouraging creativity and innovation.

Scones possess the magical ability to elevate special celebrations. By customizing scones to fit the occasion, attending to themed decoration and presentation, and orchestrating scone-centric events, you can curate unforgettable moments centered around these delectable treats.

Chapter 19: Leftover Magic: Reinventing Day-Old Scones

Giving New Life to Stale Scones

Transform day-old scones into culinary treasures with creative reinventions that breathe new life into these treats. Don't let stale scones go to waste – they hold the potential for delicious surprises.

Scone-Based Croutons, Crumbles, and More

Scone Croutons for Soups and Salads

Turn stale scones into crispy croutons that add texture and flavor to soups and salads:

Ingredients:

- Stale scones, cut into small cubes
- Olive oil
- Salt and pepper
- Optional seasonings: dried herbs, garlic powder, grated Parmesan

Instructions:

1. Preheat your oven to 350°F (175°C).
2. Toss the scone cubes with a drizzle of olive oil and your choice of seasonings.
3. Spread the cubes on a baking sheet and bake for about 10-15 minutes, or until golden and crispy.
4. Use the scone croutons to top soups, stews, or salads for added crunch.

Scone Crumbles for Desserts

Repurpose stale scones into delightful crumbles for desserts:

Ingredients:

- Stale scones, crumbled
- Butter, melted
- Brown sugar
- Cinnamon (optional)
- Fresh fruit (berries, apples, peaches, etc.)

Instructions:

1. Preheat your oven to 350°F (175°C).
2. In a bowl, combine the crumbled scones with melted butter, brown sugar, and a pinch of cinnamon if desired.
3. Spread the mixture on a baking sheet and bake for about 15-20 minutes, or until golden and crisp.
4. Allow the scone crumbles to cool and use them as a topping for ice cream, yogurt, or fruit.

Zero-Waste Scone Utilization
Scone-Based Bread Pudding
Transform stale scones into a decadent bread pudding:
Ingredients:

- Stale scones, cubed
- Milk
- Eggs
- Sugar
- Vanilla extract
- Optional mix-ins: chocolate chips, dried fruit, nuts

Instructions:

1. Preheat your oven to 350°F (175°C) and grease a baking dish.
2. In a bowl, whisk together milk, eggs, sugar, and vanilla extract.

3. Place the cubed scones in the greased baking dish and pour the milk mixture over them.
4. Gently press down to ensure the scones absorb the liquid.
5. Add any optional mix-ins and gently mix.
6. Bake for 30-35 minutes, or until the pudding is set and the top is golden.

Don't discard leftover or stale scones – embrace the magic of reinvention. From scone croutons that elevate soups and salads to scone crumbles that embellish desserts, these innovative uses ensure that no scone goes to waste. With zero-waste scone utilization, you can turn stale scones into delectable creations that surprise and delight.

Chapter 20: Creative Twists: Sweet and Savory Scone Innovations

Pushing the Boundaries of Scone Creations

Embark on a culinary adventure as we delve into the world of sweet and savory scone innovations. By pushing the boundaries of traditional scone recipes, you'll discover new and exciting ways to enjoy these beloved treats.

Unexpected Flavor Profiles and Textures

Blueberry-Lemon Basil Scones

Ingredients:

- 2 cups all-purpose flour
- 1/4 cup granulated sugar
- 1 tablespoon baking powder
- 1/2 teaspoon salt
- 1/2 cup cold unsalted butter, cubed
- 1/2 cup fresh blueberries
- Zest of 1 lemon
- 2 tablespoons finely chopped fresh basil
- 3/4 cup milk (dairy or plant-based)
- 1 teaspoon vanilla extract

Instructions:

1. Preheat your oven to 400°F (200°C) and line a baking sheet with parchment paper.
2. In a mixing bowl, whisk together the flour, sugar, baking powder, and salt.
3. Add the cold, cubed butter and work it into the dry ingredients until the mixture resembles coarse crumbs.

4. Stir in the fresh blueberries, lemon zest, and chopped basil.
5. Pour in the milk and vanilla extract. Mix gently until the dough forms.
6. Turn the dough out onto a floured surface, shape into a circle, and cut into wedges.
7. Place the scones on the baking sheet and bake for 15-18 minutes, or until golden.
8. Let cool before serving.

Encouraging Culinary Experimentation
Savory Gouda and Caramelized Onion Scones
Ingredients:

- 2 cups all-purpose flour
- 1 tablespoon baking powder
- 1/2 teaspoon salt
- 1/2 cup cold unsalted butter, cubed
- 1 cup grated Gouda cheese
- 1/2 cup caramelized onions
- 1/4 cup chopped fresh chives
- 3/4 cup milk (dairy or plant-based)

Instructions:

1. Preheat your oven to 400°F (200°C) and line a baking sheet with parchment paper.
2. In a mixing bowl, whisk together the flour, baking powder, and salt.
3. Add the cold, cubed butter and work it into the dry ingredients until the mixture resembles coarse crumbs.
4. Stir in the grated Gouda, caramelized onions, and chopped chives.
5. Pour in the milk and mix gently until the dough forms.
6. Turn the dough out onto a floured surface, shape into a circle, and cut into wedges.
7. Place the scones on the baking sheet and bake for 15-18 minutes, or until golden.
8. Let cool before serving.

Explore the art of sweet and savory scone innovations by experimenting with unexpected flavor profiles and textures. From blueberry-lemon basil scones that meld vibrant fruit and fragrant herbs to savory Gouda and caramelized onion scones that combine cheese and onions in a delightful twist, these creations invite you to break free from convention and embrace culinary exploration.

"The Scrumptious Scones Cookbook" has taken you on a delightful culinary journey through the world of scone making. From mastering the basics and crafting classic recipes to exploring innovative flavors and reinventing leftovers, this cookbook is a testament to the versatility and creativity that can be achieved with scones.

As you've discovered, scone making is not just about following recipes; it's about embracing the art of blending ingredients, textures, and flavors to create a treat that is both comforting and exciting. Whether you're a seasoned baker or a novice in the kitchen, this cookbook has provided you with the tools, techniques, and inspiration needed to create scones that will tantalize taste buds and bring joy to any occasion.

From plain and fruity to chocolatey and savory, the diverse range of scone recipes has shown you that there's a scone for every palate. You've learned how to infuse them with fresh fruits, indulgent chocolates, aromatic herbs, and international spices. You've explored ways to cater to dietary needs, from gluten-free to vegan options, ensuring that everyone can enjoy these scrumptious treats.

But this cookbook is not just about the recipes—it's about the experience. You've discovered the joy of sipping tea alongside a warm scone, indulging in scone sandwiches for breakfast, and sharing mini scones with friends at gatherings. You've learned how to make scone-centric events special and how to transform leftovers into culinary delights.

"The Scrumptious Scones Cookbook" encourages you to let your creativity run wild in the kitchen. Experiment with flavors, adapt recipes to your preferences, and create scone variations that reflect your unique taste. Whether you're celebrating a special occasion or simply enjoying a quiet moment with a cup of tea, these scones are here to make each moment a little more delicious.

Thank you for joining us on this scone-filled adventure. May your scone baking endeavors be as delightful and rewarding as the recipes you've discovered within these pages. Happy baking, and may your scones always be scrumptious!